The Form of the Fourth

The Form
of The Fourth

MARY C FULLERSON

LONDON
STUART & WATKINS
1971

FIRST PUBLISHED IN 1971
BY VINCENT STUART & JOHN M WATKINS LTD
45 LOWER BELGRAVE STREET
LONDON SW1

© VINCENT STUART & JOHN M WATKINS LTD 1971

MADE AND PRINTED
IN GREAT BRITAIN BY
WESTERN PRINTING SERVICES LTD
BRISTOL

SBN 7224 0118 3

Contents

Contents

Introduction

IN TROUBLED times we yearn to know what lies ahead. We yearn to see in order to prepare.

Yet if prophetic sight is ever sought, ever it is suspect, and rightly so. Events of major consequence seldom lack correct foretelling, but charlatans speak, too. Whether false prophets cry, "Peace, peace" where there is no peace, or "Doom, doom" when it does not apply, the falsity itself is the tragic thing.

And how to tell?

"Try the spirits, whether they be of God" becomes the earnest exercise. Try the spirit of the prophet for purity of motive, and try the spirit in ourselves as seekers of the prophet's word. Those who want but truth—for sake of truth—can learn to recognize the sound of certainty on either side. Indeed, in cloudless purity of motive there is a more dependable gauge than any found in scepticism, or even in neutral caution, by fact of our strange bias towards the dour, which makes grim ends seem surer than beneficent ones. It is the serene aggregate of seership, formed from every wisdom, every culture, which sights along the brave march all men take, to see the essential good, despite the ill.

In this book it says: "The spirit of prophecy has always had to warn, but it holds confidence for the way to come. It does not speak in terms of doubt or terror. Look up, indeed, for thy salvation draweth nigh—and to all who

will, on grander, broader scale than ever known before."
The book is about the Prophet Daniel, and what he said
concerning this, our time.

"The Book of Daniel is the book of the New Age.
Search within it for truths not realized before. It is more
than history or even prophecy; it is a blueprint of instruction for men now."

These words, and the rest which make the Preface,
were heard inwardly one morning while I sat in quiet,
meditative prayer. They were not prompted by what I
had been thinking. Except for the familiar parts about a
fiery furnace and a lions' den, I scarcely knew the story
of Daniel.

I turned to read and found the rousing narrative of
four intrepid men whose examples would serve well when
there were need for personal courage; beyond that there
seemed little to relate to any of the problems we have
today.

Nevertheless, in those first words—especially in the
way they had been said—was valid sign of supersensible
demand. I'd had its sort put to me before. I knew it was
a thing that I would do.

And so the search began, and lasted many months, and
filled many notebooks while I listened for an hour or
more every morning. There is no dreaminess about the
experience of hearing inwardly, no lack of full, clear consciousness. One must be especially alert to make an accu-
rate record, the while participating, as in any learning

process, by thinking about the concepts which are being given. As questions come to mind, they are either answered at once or dealt with later in better sequence; they are never ignored. Above all, the listener is constrained to practise in his daily life whatever may be applicable, for there is loaded danger in false mysticism that seeks no more than aimless interludes of fanciful communion. Concentrated investigation of some particular, as here, requires the disciplined, orderly quest of listening, learning, *living*, to prove the purported source, to try the spirit for reliable intent.

There are twelve chapters in the Book of Daniel. Six were basis for this volume; six are for the next. The first book in the trilogy, BY A NEW AND LIVING WAY, although prophetic in less obvious degree, also belongs to the central theme of proper preparation for what lies ahead in man's new time—a prospect which, according to these texts, is stern enough to challenge every serious heart, yet ultimately quite radiant in promise for mankind.

M.C.F.

Then Nebuchadnezzar the king was astonied, and rose up in haste, and spake, and said unto his counsellors, Did not we cast three men bound into the midst of the fire? They answered and said to the king, True, O King. He answered and said, Lo, I see four men loose, walking in the midst of the fire, and they have no hurt; and the form of the fourth is like the Son of God.

DANIEL 3: 24, 25

Preface

THE BOOK of Daniel is the book of the New Age. Search within it for truths not realized before. It is more than history or even prophecy; it is a blueprint of instruction for men now.

Look for guidance about bodily wellbeing in the situation which you face. You can be stronger than ever, even though adverse effects of man's unwisdom ever mount. And when the saturation is complete, there will be the experience of the furnace.

For New Day and the children of New Day are to come from the mouth of furnace. The Son of God will walk within it to preserve what is acceptable unto Him. But all that is not of God will be destroyed.

The world is on fire, but the Fire of My Spirit is at work as well as the fire of evil. The dross is being consumed. What is not of Me is being shaken, shaken.

Prepare for time of trial, but do not fear. Behold the way of deliverance is open before you. Hear the words of the prophet Daniel who speaks again for your day when the mountain of evil is high and distress is upon all. Look to the Son of God Who is the Way—*the Form of the Fourth* Who walks within the furnace of man's test.

Story

WHEN BABYLON'S King Nebuchadnezzar besieged and took Jerusalem, he ordered the finest children of Judah to be brought as captives to his court—children from ruling families, well favoured in appearance, poised in bearing, and skilled in all the knowledge of their land. He put a prince in charge of them and decreed that they be taught the language of Chaldaea, nurtured on the king's own fare of meat and wine, and made worthy to stand before his presence.

Among these children were four boys who were friends: Daniel, Hananiah, Mishael, and Azariah. The prince changed their names to Belteshazzar, Shadrach, Meshach, and Abednego.

Soon Belteshazzar (Daniel) decided that the king's rich food was not good for them. He asked the prince to give them vegetables and water. The prince replied that meat and wine had been decreed and if they came to look less healthy than the rest, his own head would be endangered by the king's wrath.

But Daniel had purposed in his heart not to harm his body in this way. He asked if they might have the simpler food for just ten days and then be judged by their appearance. This was agreed upon and it was found they far surpassed the children who had meat and wine. Thereafter it was granted them to eat as they desired.

While the four progressed in learning, they evidenced

other skills above the rest, and Daniel was able to interpret dreams and visions. At last when they were brought before the king, none of the captive boys could compare with Daniel, Shadrach, Meshach, and Abednego. Nebuchadnezzar was astonished at their excellence and even pitted them against mature magicians and astrologers; but the children proved ten times better in all matters of wisdom and understanding. So they remained within the king's household and grew to manhood there.

In those days, dreams were realized to be of great significance and wise men of the court were expected to interpret them. Nebuchadnezzar dreamed a dream which troubled him. When he called his chief counsellors to give its meaning, they said, "Tell it to us and we will." But the dream itself had gone from the king's mind. Only his sense of dread remained. Nevertheless he demanded that they tell him the dream he had forgot, as well as what it meant, or they would all be killed.

The counsellors were dismayed. They replied that none on earth could tell the meaning of a dream unless the dream itself be known. Only the gods, whose dwelling is not with man, could reveal such things. In rage the king decreed the death of every wise man in the realm.

Daniel and his friends were of that order now and so they were called out to be destroyed with the rest. But Daniel went directly to the king to ask for time to give him both the dream and its interpretation. Then Daniel sought his friends to pray with him that God make known the secret.

2

It was shown him in the night, and Daniel rose up with great thanksgiving, blessing the Name of God "who gives His wisdom unto men and opens the deep and hidden things and gives them light". Then he found the captain of the guards who was ready to carry out the order of death. He assured the captain that he could satisfy the king's demand.

When Daniel stood before the king, he said, "None of your sorcerers, or magicians, or astrologers could have told this thing which you desire, but there is a God in heaven who reveals mysteries. Nor has understanding been given me because of wisdom in myself more than in any other man. It is given because God wants to make known in this way what will come to pass in the latter days."

Then Daniel told the king that in his dream he had seen an enormous image, bright and terrible, composed of gold, silver, brass, iron and clay, and that while the image towered before him, a stone, cut without hands, rose up and struck it and the image crumbled and blew away as if it were chaff. But the stone became a great mountain and filled the earth!

This, Daniel said, was a foretelling of things to come. The parts of the body of the image, wrought in different metals, were different kingdoms of dominion which would follow, and in the days which corresponded to the feet of iron, mixed with clay, God Himself would set up a kingdom which shall never be destroyed, for the government of it shall not be left to others, but it shall break into pieces all lesser kingdoms and consume them.

3

Nebuchadnezzar knew this was his dream, and he believed in the interpretation Daniel gave. He bowed to him and said, "Of a truth it is that your God is a God of gods and a Lord of kings and a revealer of secrets, seeing that thou couldst reveal this secret." Then he decreed that Daniel should rule over Babylon and be made chief of the wise men whose lives he saved.

But Daniel asked that Shadrach, Meshach, and Abednego be appointed to govern the province, and that he be allowed to remain at the gateway of the king.

The king's humility was not long-lived. Soon he ordered an image of great size to be fashioned of gold and placed upon an open plain. He sent for every leader of the province to attend the dedication. When they were gathered, a herald proclaimed: "To you and all the peoples it is commanded that at the hour you hear the sound of any music you must fall down and worship the image of gold which the King Nebuchadnezzar has set up. And whosoever does not do this shall be cast into the midst of a fiery furnace."

By this time the native leaders had grown jealous of the men from Judah and watched for chances to betray them. So they reported to the king that Shadrach, Meshach, and Abednego were not obeying his decree. In rage the king called for them and demanded answer whether they served his gods and worshipped the golden image. If they did, all was well; if not they would be cast into the fire. "And then", he stormed, "who is that god who shall deliver you out of my hands?"

The three stood quietly before the irate king. Calmly they replied, "If it be so, our God whom we serve, is able to deliver us and He will. But even if not, we will not serve thy gods, nor worship the golden image."

Then the king's fury was terrible. He ordered the furnace heated seven times its usual heat and had the strongest soldiers bind them and thrust them into the fire. Flames leaped from the opening, killing the guards, while Shadrach, Meshach, and Abednego fell into the blazing pit.

Somewhat later Nebuchadnezzar approached the door to look inside. He turned in great astonishment and said to the counsellors who had plotted this, "Did we not cast three men bound in the midst of the fire?" They answered, "True, O king." But Nebuchadnezzar cried, "Lo, I see four men loose, walking in the midst of the fire, and they have no hurt; and the form of the fourth is like the Son of God!"

Then he went closer and called out: "Shadrach, Meshach, and Abednego, ye servants of the most high God, come forth." They came and stood before the king, and all could see that the fire had had no power upon their bodies, not was their hair singed, nor their clothing scorched, nor even the smell of smoke upon them. Only the cords which bound them had been burned away.

So once again the mercurial Nebuchadnezzar blessed the God in whom the Israelites had trusted. He praised the courage of the three who would not worship any god except their own, and decreed punishment of death for any who might speak a word against the God of Shadrach, Meshach, and Abednego. "For", the king said, "there is no other God that can deliver after this sort."

When Nebuchadnezzar's reign was ended, his son, Belshazzar succeeded him. One night he entertained a thousand of his lords. They drank their wine from holy vessels taken from the temple of Jerusalem. As they drank they praised the gods of gold, silver, brass, iron, wood, and stone.

But suddenly the fingers of a hand appeared and wrote four unknown words upon the plastered wall above their heads. The king was stricken with dismay and called for all the wise men of his court, promising a third of his kingdom to any who could read the writing and interpret it.

Astrologers and soothsayers came, but none of them could say what the words meant.

Then the queen told Belshazzar that there was a man in whom his father had placed especial trust. He had the spirit of light and understanding, she said, and could show the meaning of hard sentences and dissolve doubts.

So Daniel was brought before the king and promised all that was offered earlier. Daniel replied that he desired no gifts; but he would read the writing and make known its meaning.

Then in the presence of the frightened court Daniel

reminded Belshazzar of the great power his father had when he ruled Babylon, and how it had been well with him until his heart was hardened in pride, after which he lost his reason and was deposed to roam as beast, eating grass and sleeping in the fields until once more he could acknowledge that God is the true ruler of the kingdom of all men.

Daniel looked directly at Belshazzar, trembling there before him, and said, "You have made the same mistake, even though you knew this very well. You have lifted up yourself against the Lord of heaven and used the sacred vessels of the temple for wanton entertainment. You have praised the material gods, and neither seen nor heard nor known the God in whose hand your breath is. So His hand has written that your kingdom is finished and that you have been weighed in the balances and found wanting."

In that same night the king was slain. Darius of the Medes prevailed, and took the throne.

When Darius seized the kingdom from Belshazzar, he set one hundred and twenty princes over Chaldaea and above them placed three presidents, of whom he named Daniel first. Soon Darius showed such preference for Daniel that he planned to set him over the entire realm. Thereupon the other presidents and the princes sought ways to discredit him. But an excellent spirit was in Daniel; he was faithful and honest in his administration and they could find no fault. The men knew that they must seek an occasion against him concerning the law of his God.

So they went to King Darius, flattered him, and asked him to decree that for thirty days no petition be made to god or man, save to the king himself, with penalty of being cast into the den of lions. Furthermore, they pressed him to sign it according to the law of the Medes and Persians which, once made, cannot be altered.

Though Daniel knew the edict had been made and for what purpose, he went into his house, knelt as he always did three times a day before the open window facing towards Jerusalem, and offered praise to God. The princes gathered, found him praying, and hurried to report it.

Darius raged, seeing the trap he had allowed the jealous men to set. He tried to find a way to spare Daniel, but the relentless princes stood together and insisted that he honour his decree.

So the king commanded that Daniel be brought and cast into the den of lions. But he said to him, "Your God, whom you serve so faithfully, will deliver you!"

The mouth of the den was closed with a large stone and sealed, and Darius returned to the palace to spend an anxious night. Early the next morning he hurried to the den and called out, "O Daniel, servant of the living God: is thy God, whom thou servest continually, able to deliver thee?"

Daniel's triumphant voice replied, "O king, my God hath sent his angel to shut the lions' mouths and they have not hurt me."

Then Darius rejoiced and had Daniel brought up from the den. He saw that there was no harm done him because he had believed in the power of God. But the king ordered the death of the men who had plotted against Daniel. They were cast into the same den and were devoured.

Darius proclaimed that throughout the land all should recognize the God of Daniel. For he said, "He is the living God, and his kingdom shall not be destroyed and his dominion shall be even unto the end. He delivereth and rescueth; he worketh signs and wonders in heaven and in earth and hath delivered Daniel from the power of the lions."

This has been the story we are given of Daniel and his friends who proved the power of God by power of faith. And now the age of Daniel comes again. Now are the trials of his time in full similitude. Although the tests were for the few before, they test all men today. Shadrach, Meshach, and Abednego were thrust into the furnace but there was no hurt upon them for they beheld the Form of the Fourth who walked beside. Daniel was plunged into a den of lions but was not touched; an angel closed the mouths of beasts, nor did they even see him. The Form of the Fourth was there . . .

Behold the Son of God! He speaks through Daniel to His children now. Within the Book of Daniel can be found the way to walk through "furnace" and through "den of lions" and have no hurt.

See what appears again as in their time: desecration of

the sacred vessels (man's body and the natural essences of atmosphere and earth); soothsaying and claims of divination made for personal gain; worship of images of material forms; man-made decrees to limit man's freedom to worship as he would . . . betrayals, machinations, false reports . . . corruption in high places. . . .

But against it all: the power of the individual man, purified and prepared by secret dedication, to stand unharmed and unassailable. So it was for them. So it has come again that men are called to this stern preparation. And the promise is that in the tests of fire or den—fire of polluted elements and den of man's enmity towards fellow man—they shall be left entire.

For the earlier ones were prototype of many who will come to know these things in times that are upon the earth 'ere long. They will be shown a way within the Way. Daniel showed a way, and he and his three friends could walk therein to prove that the Most High was quick to bring deliverance, whether fire or lion were adversary.

For lo, I walk among men, and those who trust Me—who say, "My God *is able* to deliver me"—these shall be cast into the fire and have no hurt. Neither shall the smell of fire be upon their garments and they shall come forth purified and made ready for the kingdom to be—My Kingdom *Come*.

Do not fear. All is in My Time; all is well. Earthquakes . . . rumours of war . . . wars . . . and pestilence. . . . But do not fear. "Upon their bodies the fire had no power. . . ."

Image

So God created man in his own image, in the image of God created he him. GENESIS 1 : 27

THE IMAGE in the world today is helpless man. He has polluted the primal forces of the earth and now is sickened by its sickness and he sees no hope. Yet—in the beginning —man was made in the image of God and given dominion over every living thing.

The problem is this simple, this profound.

The image of self-will, which man has made, now towers above him as relentlessly as the image in the dream of Babylon's king, with its great head of gold. *But its feet were iron, mixed with clay!* And there arose a stone, not hewn by man—propelled as of itself—which smote the image at its feet. The mighty structure toppled, crumbled into dust, and was completely scattered by the wind. But the stone grew larger until it was a mountain. And it filled the earth.

Daniel said, "In the time which corresponds to rule of iron, mixed with clay, shall the God of Heaven set up a kingdom which shall never be destroyed, for He will Himself be ruler and that kingdom shall forever stand."

Man cannot now re-make the image he has formed, nor alter what he finds he does not like. The basic unity of life is touched and marred. Forces of mutation are already working negatively and it is over late to order change. Damage penetrates too far to legislate return to purity, or to employ any power which man can yet command and say to air and water and to soil, "Be cleansed and healed of this corruption we visited upon you when we took your gifts and exploited them without acknowledging the right to yield according to the natural rhythm of replenishment and harmonious relationship of all elements."

It is too late to do it in man's way, even in the chastened way of his repentance. He is alarmed enough to try, but it is done; man's work is done.

But God's is not! It is the time of iron mixed with clay, and there is yet the stone.

Man and the very earth were made in image of God. When man returns to his first image, he will become a son again and earth will be redeemed. This is not fanciful myth from a remote genesis, nor unrealistic promise of a visionary kind. The Son of God is Stone to break in many pieces image not of God. And the Stone will grow, and It will fill the earth. . . .

Behold the Son! Each man can be a son of this first Son, in actual fact, and in completely natural ways thus be prepared to live *in* his unnatural environment now, and *through* the coming test of earth's reaction to the outrage done to it. (Only the cords that bound them were consumed by fire.) Then he can be, as son, an agent for redemption of the earth. And God said, "Let us make man in our image, after our likeness, and let them have dominion . . . over every living thing."

But there will intervene a furnace fire's intensity to re-

12

fine the matrix of mankind for image made again in image of the Source. The ills are of such dark accumulation that he cannot live in his encasement long enough for gradual release; the desolation of the cycle will force surrender to the higher will. If conditions were more tolerable, he would not have to rise to mastery over negative force. He could dwell in shadow still. But darkness looms so powerfully that he *must* find light; and light will lead him to the planes of Son, sun of New Day, shining upon men all.

Suffer the fire of shaping. Before it falls without, let it come within to form a body tempered enough to stand when fires of radiation are too strong for physical tissue which is not prepared. The cells are being changed in children of the light. They will discover that even their skin is different; it becomes an organ of protection. (Of this the scoffer cannot know; have no concern.)

By your breath—you will be taught new mysteries of breath—you can be saved from air's pollution. By eating in the spirit of evolved thanksgiving, food will be transformed within and brought to purity. And when you would think there is not enough, lo there will be enough.

For a mighty famine, a mighty affliction shall fall upon the land, and great will be the suffering of the people. It shall come to all lands, all people, for this is the testing to see which man will stand in the strength of his dedication to the Most High. The earth is in travail and new life comes forth; but it comes *of* travail and despair. They have turned away from righteousness. They have

13

despoiled the temple. They have used the forces of secret strength for ills which they visited upon their brothers. They have looked to themselves, for themselves, and failed. . . . The Hosts are formed for battle.

Into the furnace of the times mankind is thrust. It is both furnace of his making and a cosmic fire to test and temper, purifying what can stand before the light of the New Day—of Kingdom Come—but bringing full destruction of all lesser things. The chance for choice has passed. The King's decree is made.

Man can reply as did the three who faced an earthly king in Babylon, with declaration of a faith so absolute that fear is lost even in the presence of the searing heat which flows from opened mouth of furnace. Or a man may quail, betraying his birthright to behold New Day and to be a part of it.

Whichever way he turns, the furnace stands before him now and he must enter it. The furnace will be earth itself; the door will be the Word in each, incarnate. If it be darkness in a man, darkness will fall upon him, but if light, it will be Light as never known before. Behold a New Jerusalem, indeed, and sons of God to walk with Son of God.

And I shall bring the third part through the fire and will refine them as silver is refined and will try them as gold is tried; they shall call on My Name and I will hear them; I will say, It is my people and they shall say, The Lord God is my God.

ZECHARIAH 2: 2–3

14

Behold the earth will be visited by Light of cosmic fire and those of Light shall be drawn as to a magnet in the band of light which spirals over earth. It will quicken and destroy in a single moment. "Two shall be grinding in a field . . ." What *is* of Light in essence will be pulled into a new magnetic field and made of it, and what is not will be shattered in the instant of impact.

Yea, changes upon earth itself, but men must be prepared within and not be tempted to run here or there thinking it safer in geography. Safety is *in* a man and his awareness— in his capacity to stand in midst of flame because he is the temple of the Holy Fire of My Baptism. When every cell is quickened in My Light, a man can stand entire in furnace testing, being of one Element henceforth.

Behold the searing holocaust. But those who have known the primal Fire of God within will move amid the flames of wide destruction and arise as phoenix to the bright New Day.

Worthy of test . . . work that you be made worthy of the test. Prepare but do not fear. Rout fear. The spirit of prophecy has always had to warn, but it holds confidence for the way to come. It does not speak of doom in terms of doubt or terror. "Look up, indeed, for thy salvation draweth nigh"—and on a grander, broader scale than ever known before. The ages meet in far fulfilment. Why so many now embodied? Many have joined from many eras past to meet the earth experience of New Day and from it rise to far extended planes.

Yes, man has done this thing (brought pollution and failed in brotherhood) and it is evil, but it will be used to force him higher on the plane of life. He can no longer live without the quickening which will lift him past the dangers of his own devising. It is now again as in first Garden time; he disobeyed and had to leave the effortless state of being he knew there. But when he enters Garden next, he will be larger in his spirit for having first gone out. He will have learned to be a son, indeed, by having learned the way of Very Son, and seen His Form, and found true Image there.

"He who has seen Me has seen the Father." I am the Form of the image which man can be as son. IN Me a son *is* Image of God, able to manifest entire against the image of the world, and stand despite the thrust of anything man-made. And he becomes, in turn, the crucible of transmutation for all else that is less than pure. Pure in his likeness of Creator, he makes pure whatever touches him without.

But this each man must prove as Daniel proved, as Meshach proved. It cannot be accepted only by the mind and be enough for any test. It is by BE-ing in the Image, as they were, that power is given to embody Light.

The Age of Sonlight dawns and with it power to transmute error forced upon the natural realms, upon the earth and all its life and ethers which surround it. Man has been the prodigal in distance and in darkness and returns to Light by way of Son to Father's Mansion, Garden of the sun.

When prodigal man can say in truth, "I give my will to be in image once again . . . I *will* arise and go into My Father's House . . ." then all is given back with eagerness. Even more is pressed upon the son returned than he was conscious of having had before—returned to Image, worthy of the Father . . . ready to live as citizen of New Day.

Fire

*And he looked, and behold, the bush burned with fire
and the bush was not consumed.* EXODUS 3: 2

JOHN THE BAPTIST said: "I indeed baptize you with water
unto repentance, but he that cometh after me . . . shall
baptize you with fire!" . . . the fire of the transfiguration
. . . fire of Light.

This will be His Sufficiency in time of need. It is the
Transfigured One Himself Who stands, and those who
have known the counterpart of His Transfiguration will
be left in full awareness after the searing test, for they can
bear the heat of dissolution and stand amid the flames to
be an active part of the new forming earth.

It was the quality and quantity of Fire within which
made the furnace powerless to harm the earlier ones.
Greater was Fire within than fire without. It could affect
what bound them, being not of them, not of their
essence; but even clothing which had drawn from essence
was untouched.

Fire in this intensity is Light.

Too long have men read scriptural accounts of the
experience of Light as if it could not come to ordinary
ones. They think of Shadrach or of Paul; they think of
Christ Himself, standing in that effulgence, as being in a
state almost unreal, or certainly unattainable. And yet He
said, "I am the Light of the world; he that followeth
Me shall not walk in darkness but *shall have* the light of

18

life . . .' Light that is greater than sunlight . . . Sonlight of Transfiguration . . . Holy Fire. He offers us the fire of *this* Baptism:

> When I stood transfigured, My Form was quickened by the Fire of God's pure Presence—primal Fire of the Creator. In every man the spark of this abides, waiting to be allowed to flame throughout his being. When this occurs, each cell of physical structure is transformed and filled with light and thus prepared to be untouched by lesser fire than Fire of Presence, Light of Very God. Upon the Mount the robes were shining white—the all-in-One. My Transfiguration was a time of manifested Whiteness which cemented the potential for all men. All *can* become the all-in-One *because* I AM.

When Paul had sun-experience of the Son upon Damascus Road, the Light which broke upon him was the solar Light of Logos, and the Word became a sound within his being. He could see and hear thenceforth.

In time, each soul will know this cosmic thing. This is the age of wide initiation. In the coming test, many will have the birth of Christ within, but those who *stand* in midst of flame and see beside them there the radiant Son —these will be taken through the portal of a transformation into Light of *BE*-ing. Then the transfigured ones will lead the people in whom the Christ be born. The Shining One Himself will be the ultimate head and when His government has come, the land will lie in peace and breathe in beauty, and men can walk in inner power towards even higher births. New Life of the New Day will be beyond man's farthest dream of life as it is known before he opens to the One Who gives him Life as son of Son.

The world needs to re-learn the way of Light in great simplicity as it was given by the Word Himself—Logos of God: the clear and blinding concept of the FACT of God in Light, and light in man; and Son of God *as* Son of Man, standing between to reconcile the difference in intensity.

When Peter and James and John beheld the Light of the Transfigured One with Moses and Elias, they thought to build earth tabernacles, as men always do, trying to make an outer edifice when the temple is there in man himself—*temple*, indeed. *Man* is to be the temple, and *let* the Light of the Transfiguration flame upon the altar of his heart. Then he is infused with light stronger and brighter, heated beyond the heat of any lesser thing.

And now, albeit unseen, we walk with giants of Presence Who have known the time of Fire. They come with swords to cut away our doubt and our reluctance to believe that we can experience Light in this degree within the human, physical frame . . .

We must not fear. "Fear not!" is always said to those who stand before the presence of a Messenger of Power. Fear not in the frail vehicle of flesh to be confronted by the promise of the quickening required.

Ever through time there have been occasions when man's spirit soared to experience Light in its pure essence, but his body could not dwell in such intensity. Earth's evolution was not ready. He returned to say, "I saw; I felt; I *know*", but he could only let the blinding light be taken from his eyes or they were sightless for the forms of living he returned to. Now he will be allowed to realize Light in every part of being and endure. The vehicle will be fused into an image which can perfectly support the Very Light of God.

When true baptism by water is performed, the heart is dedicated; but *will* is given when it comes by Fire. It is the point of latent fire in dedicated will—in human will, surrendered to the Will of God—which meets the Fire of Transfiguration from above; and in the mighty moment of its contact, man's finite spirit is fused into the Image. Surrendered, quickened will *is* transfiguration. This is the core of the experience as far as man is capable of receiving it in conscious being.

Behold I baptize with Fire and by the Rod. When Moses used his rod to smite the rock, water came forth as sign. Water has ever been the sign of preparation . . . "as in the days of Noah" . . . water dissolving what would not yield to the dynamic of conversion . . . baptism by water, cleansing, making ready for the higher thing of BE-ing when spirit can be fired by Presence. I lay the Rod of Fire upon the one who *will* be son of Son—of sun and Light. Shekinah! Let it come. This is the glory of the Lord men prate about, but each must have within to know without. I call to man in terms of his first-fire. I would have him know the burning bush within. Out of the unconsuming Fire, the promise of his full deliverance comes.

21

Thus in the beginning; thus it shall be again. Man will return, remembering his former state, but he must let it be recovery in fullness of his being. He must, with simple dedication, as Daniel did, suffer the disciplines that refine the vessel into which the Form be poured. Physical structure must be purified for fire of spirit which will fall upon man now, unit by unit, to become the new race of men, children of New Day, sons of the Son of God.

The glands have long been mystery. Doctors know their power but not their heart. They do not know that centres of Holy Fire are there to keep the spirit of God alive in man. Some only feebly burn, but when a conscious act of will-surrender is made, the flame leaps up and quickens every atom of the body. Light then indwells, posited in the glands, to flow throughout the being. When mankind as a whole has come to live entirely in the Will-of-God, his physical appearance will have changed and he will be immune to any danger from outside himself.

In the Book of Daniel we find practical ways to prepare for this. By means of ritual, to be considered next, and by specific disciplines, given subsequently, we can learn to offer readiness. But attributes and attitudes are dealt with first. We must believe we *can* be conscious son. Then we begin to be.

Nor does mastery come until one seeks the Son because He *is* the Son, and not that he, as son, may find perfection or protection. Selfhood as a son must first be lost in sight of total Son. Unless there be surrender, the urge to command perfection has inherently grave danger. Upon surrender to the Ascended Christ, the Spirit of Resurrection becomes the actual empowering for the process of regeneration; the work is done *by* Fire of Spirit. Even the physical cells are Son-ed in sun of dedicated will.

Ritual

*For as many as are led by the Spirit of God, they are
the sons of God.* ROMANS 8: 14

IT WAS in ritual that Daniel found his quickening. For
sake of it he defied a king's decree of death, but it
enabled him to enter den of lions and leave the den
entire. When ritual is real, enlivened, it is fraught with
power. A man who lives its secret is prepared to stand.

Ritual of this degree is total sacrament. One moves
from task to task with consciousness that he belongs, as
creature, to Creator. And he meets his brother, feeling
that each encounter is a simple ceremony of approach, no
matter how prosaic be the terms of the transaction in
time or purpose.

Let every act be ritual, interior and very personal, disciplined enough to do with faithfulness, yet not so rigidly
established that it turns to lifeless form. When attitude of
ritualistic living enters deeply into our desire, we *become*
the living ritual itself. Of this order it is then true prayer
—the prayer of consummate being, the genesis of overcomer.

There follow here suggestions for this way of life. It
is unlikely that they will all appeal to everyone, but the
essential attitude towards ritual can be found in them.
Several may seem suitable for a while and then a different
set be chosen. Or we may be given wholly personal ones
—known to no one else—which will become our secret

strength. Better the ones each finds because he turns direct to be receiver for himself . . . the way he may rise from his bed, open a door, regard the morning sky. . . . They will be simple, simpler than those common now, but filled with greater potency, being alive and newly felt and seen.

The important element is that at each time of use our choice be made by quickening from within. Ritual without awareness is not only dead but deadening. We cannot go through the motions of an unfelt rite without receiving actual harm. We cannot make a graven image even of forms we take for worship. The single eye . . . the chalice of sincerity . . . these we must bring the altar from within.

And so it is that rituals given here are patterns of intent rather than ceremonial postures or formulae of sound. They must not lead to compliance so inflexible that poise is lost when circumstances hinder planned observance. If performance cannot be entire or actual, then let it be projected from a symbol, or be imagined without any tangible form. Vital symbolism represents reality of interchange, used only in conscious union with the inspiration for it.

The age of enlightened ceremony dawns. Lifeless forms of decoration, dead forms in ceremony—these will all be left in the heap discarded by New Day's thought. Nothing but quickened beauty and true life will satisfy when new man comes to stand within the gateway of the King.

Ritual of Sufficiency

*If it be so, our God whom we serve is able to deliver
us from the burning fiery furnace, and he will deliver
us out of thine hand, O king.* DANIEL 3: 17

THINK OF the three. Think of the three. They said, "If
it be so, our God, whom we serve, is able to deliver us."
These had so lived in the conviction of Sufficiency that
in the time of test even their bones and muscles were
imbued with faith that was impervious to fire.

This is the first interior action asked of us: that we
bring all our being into focus to believe that God's
original plan for His creation will not fail, and that God
IS, whatever test be met.

Lo, I call you to stand in the spirit of Shadrach, Meshach,
and Abednego and *know* that your God is able to prevail
against the lesser fires of man. Believe and thus become
impervious—not that you be saved, not for the sake of
being saved, but that God's plan be saved in you.

Prepare by meditation upon the power to say: "If it
be so . . ." Sense the wonder of the experience these
three men had in the furnace of the king. Let it well up
within as profoundest praise—for the beauty of their
Abraham-like obedience, their awesome faith, and the
magnificence of their deliverance. . . . Into the furnace
they could take pure love of God, and draw the Son
Himself, the Form of the Fourth, to walk beside them

26

there in His Sufficiency. They offered unfaltering trust, and it was met entire by Overcomer. These are the poles of full protection: the faith required to draw the Overcomer for the overcoming.

Never try to stand in your own strength. Christ-sufficiency is the secret of the power to stand. This total consecration was the stalwart shield for Daniel and his friends. Everything they did, and every day, was hammered strong by dedication and by faith in God.

Pray thus: God of Shadrach, Meshach, and Abednego, help me to perceive their faith, the strength of their commitment, the shield of their certainty that "If it be so", Your power can deliver me. Grant me their faith.

For, remember, Faith *is* a gift! One asks, in faith, that Faith be his by grace. By grace of God man's faith will draw the Faith to stand and *let* himself be strong enough to stand! If only the great reciprocal action between God and man, man and God, were realized and allowed by man! Freewill was given him that he might learn to give it back to God and thus receive the ALL he so requires. Soon he will find he can no longer live without faith enough to experience Faith!

Look to Me only for instruction. That keeps you pure in knowledge. Look to Me only for the love which you must hold towards others. That keeps you pure in wisdom. Look to Me only for the empowering during trials to come. That keeps you in right strength. Then relax and let Me do this work in you. Let My peace come into you . . . Let My protection surround you . . . *Discover* My Sufficiency!

27

The assurance you will come to know will be like that of Daniel and his friends. As it was for them, it is now for you: threat of den and furnace, symbolic of the fierce, destructive thought and damaging action in your world. Stay careless of effect, but ever deepen confidence that you, as unit of mankind, can be preserved and changed to better form.

This is the Ritual of Sufficiency: to live in flawless certainty of God. . . .

Ritual of Equilibrium

*Take my yoke upon you, and learn of me . . . and ye
shall find rest unto your souls . . . For my yoke is
easy, and my burden is light.* MATTHEW 11: 29, 30

WHEN WE learn to know that Christ is our sufficiency,
there is equilibrium. In balanced relationship to God and
man, we rest. Neither stimulated by the forward look, nor
weighted by a backward glance, we accept the present
moment. With no preponderance of mind or heart—too
much of thinking, too much of feeling—we are poised
in spirit.

Then the peace we know is not quiescence; it is the
balanced power of governed effort, of pivotal control at
the point where Presence within us meets Presence without in any situation, any circumstance.

As Ritual of Equilibrium, stand and in imagination
form a cross. Feel awareness centred where the beams are
joined. Let all sense of past leave consciousness; let all
thought of future be withheld. Let over-balance towards
emotion or towards thinking be levelled at the crossbeam.
Then feel that there the Christ-of-Presence rests. Take
very quiet breath—slow and deep and certain—and go
from this position with evenness of step. *Sustain* the
dignity of equilibrium.

We can be held in exquisite balance upon the Cross of
Presence, yoked to the Christ within . . .

Take My yoke upon you. Feel its strength and its incredible
lightness. Balance beneath it and walk with steady pace . . .

Ritual of Rest

There remaineth therefore a rest to the people of God . . . HEBREWS 4: 9

THE SPIRIT of the Presence comes to say:

My Rest! The beauty, the order, the serene rightness of it. But so few know to seek it or will accept it. It is an activity of self to resist—to want to do, do, do with human strength. You seek gadgets to ease your work but do not use My Rest, available within.

Rest in Me means poise in Me—a Centredness from which all action starts: action of mind, of heart, of body. It is not weak submissiveness; it is vibrant poise, full of the energy of abundant Life.

Rest in Me is the deep Centredness of total being, more than ease of body or of mind which "rest" connotes to weary man; yet it prevents weariness even of these, for the cell that is without self-stress feeds directly upon Me and is quickened there.

As Ritual of Rest identify with bark, with silent snow, with nature's coverings, with hulls of seeds. There is a winter work to do deep at the core. There will be stir of roots extending down . . .

At core of being at first there seems no further thing to feel, to hear; there is such toneless peace, such deep passivity. And one should wait awhile in Centred essence there.

Then accept the charge of power which can be held

within the citadel of peace. Open the door above and let the wonder come to race down all the corridors of blood, from head to heart, through lungs to arms and legs, and then to deep, interior organs. Let energy circulate as conscious flow throughout the body, but be sure that the core of being is quiet—*very* still.

The avenue of energy is the quiet joy of rest, where mind and body and spirit are made one in Me. Then let what may offend you from without; thy sanctuary dwells secure . . . the walls of thy awareness are blessed by strength; nothing can invade your peace.

And if you should be tempted to forget, be great in the humility of returning to this Rest. Blessed are the meek— the disciplined ones who can say to their uneasy thought, "Go into obedience, be purified in Light, and be serene in Peace."

Look at the unutterable darkness about you and lift up your head to glory in the Light. It is coming with such force to penetrate all hidden things that you sense its terrible thrust, and when uncentred, it brings intolerable unrest. Rest, rest, but without rest! Deal with unrest by act of will unto the higher Will—by surrender, instant by instant, to the Centre-core of peace . . . asleep in the boat in midst of tempest because your consciousness is totally awake before the throne of My Security!

. . . When enough have entered into the Sabbath of Rest, man will be ready to live in redeemed conditions, and the world will be changed.

Ritual of Becoming

Consider the lilies how they grow: they toil not, they spin not . . . LUKE 12: 27

Consider the lilies how they *grow*: they toil not, neither do they spin . . . but I say to you they are arrayed in BE-ing: they *are* in Me. Their stillness is not static in its centredness. It is a moving worship too serene to see.

In BE-ing all is done. When at the door of creation My Word was "Let!" all was accomplished for fulfilment of *to be*. Creation continues in its BE-ingness, and this is also Law for the development of man. When you can be in Me in all things, all things will be unto you as *of* Me.

I speak then by permeation. You "hear" Me as KNOW-ING, as identification, as the dignity of perfect Law, the uncluttered Creed. Theological quibblings set men back so far. You need but live a single truth of BE-ing until it IS within. Then there is no reason for theology as men think of it! You have *become* the study of God—the Word of God within.

The Word is meant to live, to BE in each. And the Word was made flesh *in* Me, and *from* Me into every son who will. Each cell is son, and as each son, is Son!

THE WONDER of Creation—the blest birth . . . Identify with grass. Pulse with the earth; breathe with the bark of trees . . . Let all that IS find all that IS within yourself and find it good. There is no barrier to the interchange of LIFE. Then look and you will see; listen and you will hear the very sound of borning and of BE-ing in all things. The so-called secrets are no secrets then. You *know*! Nature will bend before your eye. She will remove her coverings and let you see. You will be one with her and then dominion promised comes, indeed.

Many glimpse the outer courts of this pure state of being, but mistake the way to enter. Turning inward, they turn inward selfishly. One does not come that way. One comes into the inner place, holy of holies, as priest of high awareness for the ALL—all-of-all, and unto ALL —not to be lost in nothingness without sensation, but to find completion in the whole as a perfected unit.

Unity means oneness in the highest way—and man can seldom grasp its meaning even enough to strive towards it, *until* he turns in such humility of dedication that he forgets to seek a way for his own growth and loses his identity in ALL, in dedication to the ALL. Then the way opens and he finds he has not lost his special self-ness when he came. It is intensified!

This is a ritual of development which none can hasten. In its time within the being, BE-ing comes. You watch the caterpillar change its skin the many times, each time becoming larger for its task of transformation in the dark cocoon; and then you see its coming forth to live with wings in the new dimension of the air—the same identity, yet not the same, bearing natural growth, natural progression, to the next intended phase of life expression. If My children could accept the *naturalness* of BE-ing unto Me, it would be less a straining to achieve and more of letting this occur. Placed in nature's wisdom where it can thus

33

grow, the caterpillar eats and thrives upon the food at hand. It grows and waits for larger skin, and eats and grows again. Nature can teach you through this creature that is obedient to the thrust of Life within, but moves with patience towards the farther time when it can leave the crawling stage and fly. BE-ing is the butterfly, the moth. . . .

BE-ing in Me you "fly" in consciousness, but having been prepared to move upon the air it is a natural life. There is no strain. You are not meant to reach this stage until it is not strange to be there! At home in Me—in My dimension—because you have allowed Me to BE-come in you.

Remember there are intimations in the crawling stage of what lies ahead. Sometimes a soul, foreseeing, grows impatient and wants to fly too soon. You watch the moth, wings folded, standing to let them dry, then gradually extend and stiffen before attempted flight. They move by instinct and it is well with them, but the human mind can interfere; the human will can leap ahead demanding what it should not have too soon.

Development is safe and natural done *in* Me. I came to BE the Way—in kind, in time—for every man. Let there be a ritual of remembering the way of chrysalis and butterfly, of cocoon and moth. . . . The work of transformation is done well in its secret chambers. The caterpillar trusts and enters total quietness of BE-ing that it may come forth as a winged one, wholly changed.

When personal desire and personal will are offered to the Whole; when there is so little left of thought for outcome on self-level that it is scarcely to be considered, then use is made by ALL and unto all. Even in times when no apparent action is occurring, action IS. BE-ing is forming, waves of power are moving in and out. . . .

I call you to be willing, then, to BE. BE-ing is the great use, the pure use, the powerful use. Regeneration can occur on grandest scale when enough will have *become* in this degree.

Ritual of True Praise

And it shall come to pass that from one new moon to another, and from one sabbath to another, shall all flesh come to worship before me, saith the Lord.
ISAIAH 66: 23

OUT OF the spirit of praise comes power and shield; praise is protector but it must be true.

Man has long thought devotion could be shown by churchly forms on a particular day. He will soon find it does not serve in face of fire or den. It will not be enough to turn the judgment when he stands in field—"two grinding there . . ."

Devotion means living unto God—no breath apart from being unto Him, no ambition but to be acceptable and pure and harmless in the grace of world made manifest, as brother of all life because God is the Father of each blade of grass which trembles under foot. The killer shall be killed unless he learns.

Praise is the generator and the insulator of the sensitive core. When every action comes from Centre, man is safe no matter what the test. Centre is kept in Light by perfect praise.

Daniel and his friends were ever mindful of God as their Creator, and of their being bound to Him in utter obligation and dependence. By Him they came to being; by Him they lived. Their hymns of praise, their prayers of supplication, attested God's dominion, and these were

36

men most skilled in science, the most intelligent men of all the realm. It was their highest wisdom to proclaim the Fatherhood of God and breathe as sons.

By disciplined body, heart, and mind, as well as spirit, they offered the pure worship of a whole devotion. Inevitably it made them powerful, but power was never sullied in its use because they knelt three times a day in formal rites of praise, and lived the other hours in highest faithfulness. Their inner being kept its altar presence at all times.

Sing silent, secret praises constantly. Real worship is abiding consciousness of God. Praise is the sound of sonship. It is the voice which speaks from will in man and lifts it to the Will of God. Will to praise and know the Will of God!

Learn to withdraw emotion from your praise—not for lack of feeling, but for feeling totally involved. Praise as a pine tree stands; praise as a bird, because of BE-ing.

For Ritual of Praise, we rise and look to East with gladness on our face towards God of sun, and Son of Morning Star, receiving full empowering for the day by literal inflow of sun-ray energy.

At noon we lift our eyes to centre sky, rejoicing in the constancy of God which stabilizes us no matter what assails or would deflect.

When evening comes we give our thanks for day and praise for night which offers purpose of repose that worship may drop deep into the cells of physical being. Pervading praise makes strong the body's tissue while we sleep, and tones and quickens organs which are stressed by fear. Praise is the attitude from which the Fire of Overcoming rises to form a shield around the body and preserve its strength within.

For deeper ritual-meditation, we trace and then identify with man's worship through the ages, with patterns and first-fires of his awareness that there was a Life beyond him which was yet within because he was of life himself, the creature made by Light from "Let!"

Recall the structures he has formed—from unhewn altar to the spire of great cathedral. Stand in bowered crypt of Indians, in kivas and in caves, and feel the lines of worship as they grow into the tower of true devotion which shall rise when man evolves to recognition of the temple that he is.

Return to courts of Greece . . . to steps of Mayan temples . . . Invoke the spirit of all places of oblation, the simple ones and those elaborate, each showing an attribute of worship and an attitude of praise. Suffer the dimness and restraint when man's self-seeking homage became his justification for cruelties and schisms. And then behold the promise of the bright redemption when he worships on the farther side of Fire. Humble and tall, chastened and triumphant, see him stand within the courts of light-filled praise.

(And this is purest worship—what takes place within the heart, with no desire to share except in unseen emanation because the Father *is* in Light within and cannot be contained.)

Come now. Enter your own temple presence and let your praise be true. Hold it in eye and body, in mind and spirit . . . in your goings and comings . . . in all you do.

The great priest of praise, King David, said:

"As for me, I will call upon God; and the Lord shall save me. Evening, and morning, and at noon will I pray, and cry aloud and he shall hear my voice."

PSALM 55: 16, 17

When man gives ritual-praise in purity of heart three times a day as Daniel did, as David, the *fourth* praise will be unto him from Power beyond! Squared the walls which encompass then his soul . . . domed the translucent roof. . . .

Ritual of the Temple Way

*Know ye not that ye are the temple of God, and that
the Spirit of God dwelleth in you?* I COR. 3: 16

THINK OF your body-temple as cathedral form. Correlate
the pattern and design, the structure, and the fittings.
Remember the intended use. Let your body worship. Let
it praise. Let songs of exultation rise within the cells.
Look *up* . . . feel the vaulted reaches. Identify with
strength in bone and sinew.

Then look about . . . your senses are the windows,
and that one of such magnificence at the farthest end—
is that not the single eye, the Eye of Spirit? "If thine eye
be single thy whole body (temple) shall be filled with
Light!" Look to that window in meditation . . . look
through the single eye to see the truth of being.

Then walk in quiet dignity down the aisles. Consider
the fluidic body . . . feel the blood and lymph in movement. Let circulation be a conscious flow. Let it be His
Blood that pulses through your being. Cleanse the etheric.
Dedicate its use. Sense the sacrament in every physical cell.

Now stand before the holy altar. Breathe Me in and know
that every aspect of your feeling and emotion can be purified and stabilized by breath—the breath of God. Work
until you hold the exquisite balance of awareness which is
very still in Me—neither too high, nor dropped too low
. . . poised in My Presence . . . unmoved by what befalls.
Then kneel in deep contemplation of the Will—the Will

40

of God in you . . . in every segment, but in the whole of
being which is now offered unto Me. Let holy heat pervade,
remembering that Will is Light and Fire, and is the ultimate
offering of the human soul. It came in its triumphant hour
for Me when in the garden I could say, "Not My will, but
Thine be done."

Learn to discern My Body in its threefold form and know
its total Temple Presence: the Body of Sacrifice (by having
come to dwell in earthly frame); the Body of Ascension
(by triumphant overcoming to make the Way for man);
and the Body of Indwelling Presence (the etheric BE-ing,
returned to *be* in each and yet in all.)*

This is the way to see My true cathedral Form. This is
the way to see yourself, as well. Man kneels, that he may
rise, that he may walk! . . . exemplifying sacrifice, ascension,
and abiding recollection.

The body of sacrifice in each of us is understood as
the physical-etheric one which must experience (suffer)
human existence to provide the form required. The body
of ascension is the individualized spirit-counterpart of the
Transfigured One, which is capable of Radiance. When it
has touched the throne of the Son-Presence, we are able,
then, to live in the third, the conscious body of sustained
awareness.

Walk today, walk every day the temple way, and put your
"bodies" on the altar there. I will accept the offering, and
return the incense of oblation to your world . . .

* The threefold manner in which the Body of Christ may be discerned
is the theme of *By a New and Living Way*, Mary C. Fullerson (Vincent
Stuart, London, 1963).

Ritual of Direct Approach

*There is a spirit in man and the inspiration of the
Almighty giveth them understanding.* JOB 32: 8

Now WHEN man sees darkness deep within and yearns
towards light, he can be taught again as he was taught
in ages past—directly by God's Spirit. This is the tenor
of our time: that many want to inquire into matters of
spirit and be told. Both light and darkness are in this
strong, new urge, but it is light that will prevail. Only
the chastened ones, whose motives have been purified,
will hear correctly. A scourge will fall on those who
exploit the desire.

Out of the divine energy of dedication, Daniel heard.
He wanted only truth to bridge the gap in consciousness
between man and God. He asked for no reward, no power.
He kept the needed disciplines in secrecy and faithfulness.
Daniel's devotion to God became his wisdom. Thus he
knew.

The Ritual of Direct Approach is a prayer and a commitment: "Lord, help me to hear aright because I have
desire for truth. Then strengthen me to walk the guided
way."

Yea, truth is born of right motive. That man who seeks to
hear that he may be instructed correctly and walk rightly,
will hear aright. But he that seeks to be known of others
as prophet and seer can be led astray and lead his followers
astray, and neither shall know until he falls into the ditch.

Indeed, the balance is so delicate a thing that even authentic inspiration, if centred long in any man, or any group, and voiced as truth *for all*, can be sullied by self-assertion or the taint of other men's acclaim.

When mankind as a whole prepares itself to listen, then can God's direct rulers, the Hosts of Heaven, walk with man and instruct him for Kingdom living in New Age. On widest scale, minds must be trained to accommodate a new capacity, and be disciplined for safe use of these extended powers, that no self-interest may defile the gift.

For knowledge of that which moves within the being of the elements, and in the cells of man's physical structure, must come of dedicated will, or there is chaos. It was because man's will was faced away from Me, that darkness entered deep into the core of manifested life. He can learn to bring perfection back into his body and estate, but only when he turns, as son, to Source of knowledge.

"The fear of the Lord is the beginning of wisdom, and the knowledge of the holy is understanding," Solomon said. As the dedicated heart becomes a sound physical organ, so the disciplined mind is made a strong and reliable servant. Nothing asked of one who has been richly endowed in mind will betray the logic of that mind, but interior truth must first be seen by eye of faith. Nor is this kind of knowing closed to any except those who try to fit it first into a mould of finite thinking.

I will satisfy the mind beyond the mind's last dream, but

43

only after it can rest before Me as a little child. It is the mind *in* Me which is the knower. Only there can man find wisdom enough even for the practical matters of his life. When you pray: "Let the Mind of Christ be in my mind," you have prayed for the whole Mind of intellectual and intuitional action—the knowing and the Knower within. And nothing less will serve you now.

Indeed, it is My time upon the earth and upon the people of the earth and upon the vapours surrounding the earth, that all be transformed and purified for Kingdom Come. Purity and quickening shall be upon the land and air and in the bodies of men. For sins of defilement have entered into these to pollute the wisdom of instinctive will. But again let each be taught directly. Instinctive knowledge can be his once more; the cells of inner being will discern.

This is the kingdom of direct approach. All may come to Me without an intercessor. None need wait. So many do not know, or will not yet believe, that I want to deal with them directly.

It was said to the people by Moses: "The Lord talked with you face to face in the mount, out of the midst of the fire, and I stood between the Lord and you at that time, to shew you the word of the Lord, for ye were afraid by reason of the fire." (Deut. 5: 4, 5)

Behold the mountain of direct approach! No more need man fear "by reason of the fire" and none need stand between him when the Lord would speak.

Ritual of Image-Forming

*And as we have borne the image of the earthy; we
shall also bear the image of the heavenly.*
1 CORINTHIANS 15: 49

ENTER THE deep, interior ritual of image-forming, the
powerful image of remembered Fire. Only the soul that
wakes to memory of its origin, begotten in the image of
God, can know its destiny to live again in ultimate consciousness as a son of God. Man was born of Fire and
will return to Fire.

Fire of first image is a constant force to quicken and
maintain the physical being, and all bodies joined, in
perfect wholeness. Furnace is but threat of lesser fire. It
cannot touch the Fire of Wholeness—white heat of
Union . . . fusion of Return.

The vision of Return: it is the image of man, made in
the Image of God. And we must see it first in the First-
Son-of-God! As First-Son stood in earth expression, He
stands now in His extended Presence as the brilliant
image of the Christed-One so that lesser sons may see
the etheric Form.

It has been said: "But as many as received him, to
them gave he power to become the sons of God . . ."
(John 1: 12). For He is Himself the WAY, and the way
for man is counterpart of the Way for Son of Man. Man
becomes a son of God by following in the way which
he could not have taken but for Very Son. Image of man

45

. . . Image of God . . . Rejoice as sons that Son can show Him thus!

In your own body you can *be* first image now. Allow it to be felt new and entire—fire of the point of first emergence, formed of the formlessness of Cause. Feel the turning of the great wheel of Creation to bring its focus to the pivot-point. Feel the mists move in circular waves towards the centre-core which can contain the spark of sentient life, and *know* it there!

Then look back and down at Earth. See it whole and beautiful—as perfect as the perfect image which was brought to dwell upon it. See the changing form of man, moving in time from point of original Light, and feel the ages turn upon the spiral while man drops farther into darkened planes apart. But ever hold the destiny complete —the ultimate transfiguration by the Fire of Son.

Enter deeply into Ritual of Image-Forming . . . Feel the perfection of first Image in you now . . .

Feel it for all mankind . . .

Ritual of the New Communion

*But I say unto you, I will not drink henceforth of this
fruit of the vine, until that day when I drink it new
with you in My Father's Kingdom.* MATTHEW 26: 29

COMMUNION IN New Day will be a *new* communion.
Whole man will come. He will identify all aspects of his
body-being directly with the Body of Transfiguration
and find renewal there. Once he has known the bright
transparency of union in the Transfigured One, he can
bear the forces of regeneration. The Son-at-Throne is
every vibration in perfection and moves unerringly towards the particular in every son of His.

Thus man will know the ritual of Communion in New
Day—an enlightened form of living power, drawn from
Centred-Source for full vitality. And for any who will
have it so, it can become a new and quickened rite today.
None need wait to be the grail for wonder of true life,
poured into the vessel of his being, held aloft in recognition of the Body of Christ.

When you seek communion, bring the symbols of this
recognition. Partake in ritual and in reality. Prepare the
unleavened bread yourself—a wafer, thinly rolled and
fired by sun! Make it of coarse milled grain, moistened
with wine and water. And use oil.

Ever since Christ's Supper was ordained, His children's
holy food has been some form of sacramental bread and
wine. With their components from the elements of air and

47

earth and water, these symbols are brought to new significance in fire—the fourth and the transforming element —and oil becomes its witness in the sacrament. It betokens conscious gladness unto God—the pulsing symbol of those sons who see the Very Son as radiant Form.

Oil enters the new rite by gesture of touch upon the centres of perception: top of head, middle of brow, upon the throat, upon heart-centre. Placed upon these outer points, oil signifies acknowledgement of His Presence standing beside, the while He abides within. For this is the greater wonder: that Christ-etheric Form not only indwells, but is perceived as permeation and as pervasion without.

Communion rite is new rite after Fire. There is knowledge of the force-field of dynamic Christ-converted beingness. This magnetic envelopment is protection from material or psychic harm. It is regeneration for tissue of body, or of mind and heart intent. It is life-changing enablement in human relationship and earth environment. It is the Furnace of Beholding in which the Form is as the Son of Man, and Son of God.

Ritual of Washing of the Feet

*So we, being many, are one body in Christ and every-
one member one of another.* ROMANS 12: 5

WHEN JESUS bent to wash the feet of His disciples, they
objected. Peter said: "Thou shalt never wash *my* feet!"
But Jesus answered, "If I wash thee not, thou hast no
part with Me."

"If I wash thee not . . ." are still His words to us. We
must be cleansed on the level at which we walk with
other men. It is not enough to have our heads held high
in realms of spiritual thought. How is it with our feet,
my friend? How is it now with them?

He said: "Ye call me Master and Lord, and ye say well;
for so I am. If I, then your Lord and Master have washed
your feet; ye also ought to wash one another's feet"
(John 13: 13, 14).

In essence this is to be done for everyone we meet.
True brotherhood is the freedom from judgment and
the humility of heart which makes it seem no task to bend
and wash the feet of anyone. It is a matter for the heart
to know and in imagination *do*—a very secret rite, as the
core of man must ever be the point of real connection
with the power of God. It is a rite done deeply in the
soul, but the highest priests of spirit will attend, and
man's whole being become Temple-arch.

Having identified with Son and Father at the Supper
of Communion, we kneel in deep communion with all

other men to cleanse and to be cleansed by pure heart-brotherhood. And in every first encounter with another we observe the Ritual of Washing of the Feet:

> When you meet, look down a moment and know within that you are *willing* to perform the act in literal obedience because you feel the wonder of My gift of Life and have accepted Blood relationship to all *because* of Me! If you cannot bend in heart to understand the fact of soil, from having walked in dust and mind of earth, and thus not shun your brother, you have no part in Me, for I indwell all men and offer all Forgiveness and Love. How, then, could you be with Me if unwilling to go with Me into every other man?—for this I do, and any who reserves his love towards others must be left outside the circuit of that course.

Behold the day has come when the full Blood relationship of man must be acknowledged and accepted as a pulsing, common Heart within the total Body, or circulation is cut off from any part restricted from the flow.

Look to thy feet, My children. How is it now with them?

Ritual of Tower Position

The Lord is my rock and my fortress . . . the horn of
my salvation, and my high tower. PSALM 18: 2

THIS IS a ritual of empowering by vision and by voice.

Before men built the Tower of Babel "the whole world
was of one language and of one speech". But the lust of
separativeness was tempting and they said, "Let us make
a tower whose top may reach to heaven, and let us make
a name, lest we be scattered abroad upon the face of the
whole earth."

As punishment for this evil against God, Who made
all men and made them one, their language was con-
founded and they lost the power to understand and speak
as one. Long ago the bricks of Babel fell; yet in its
essence who can say it is not present still?

But now stand tall and foresee the Tower of New Day,
formed of mankind itself when each shall take his place
as part of the great structure of humanity, made strong
in unassailable brotherhood. Then the many races and the
many creeds are one, and a single language can be understood once more.

Behold, it differs well from Babel's tower. There are
no spiralling steps! None climbs alone by effort; each *is*
of ALL because of willingness to meld his own advantage
within the total goal of Presence.

Lo, each of My own becomes a part of Tower in whatever

place he be, and the world will be saved by the crying unto Me from its pinnacle of Light . . . Mount high in your awareness and voice the prayer that all mankind be one unto the One, united as a tower is built towards sky, in singleness of structure, though the stones be many which make it high and strong.

Stand and face the four directions to do this speaking work. There will be knowledge for you of the power that comes of it, and joy for you in its voicing. Blessed are those who voice the Tower prayer . . .

Prayer establishes lines of Light for reaching points of need. Continued prayer makes ever stronger channels. Speak to those whom spirit spotlights for you. If need be do this silently, but with the conviction of a hearty shout! Do it with faithfulness. Wherever they may be it strengthens them. They hear. It is a matter now of soul and soul. Speak courage—*courage* is the great tower quality.

Say: "Stand fast! . . .
  "Hold steady . . .
    "Yield not . . .
      "*Be* in His Name."
Say: "Dare! . . .
  "Believe that you can . . .
    "Your daring will bear fruit."
Say: "Listen! . . .
  "Receive . . .
    "Love all . . .
      "*Come higher!*"

"Come higher" is always call, as well as answer to the needs of man. Stand high in Me that you may stand secure. In Me you can be a tower of power for those who cry in the night of despair.

From tower-position look upon the world in its torment of travail and fratricide, and envision the wonder and the good which comes when mankind puts its feet upon the Way which carries him to unity in Light of Brotherhood.

Ritual of Necessary Change

*Now we beseech you . . . that ye be not soon shaken
in mind, or be troubled, neither by spirit, nor by word,
nor by letter . . .* II THESSALONIANS 2: 1, 2

THIS IS a ritual of attitude. It is performed by thought.
Think on these things:

I am the magnet of divine unrest that Peace may come
indeed. I told My early ones to have no fear of war and
rumour, earthquake and pestilence. I tell you now again,
fear not the outer evidence of change. It can be suffered in
My Strength, behind My Shield. But fear the failure to
perceive what is at work and be a part of it, for changes
must be wrought, that spirit may be purged for freedom
on the next Light plane.

The power in change! Accept the need for change—
not with sense of loss to see forms move from stage to
stage, but with belief in growth, in evolution, in great
on-goingness. You see a caterpillar enter its cocoon, and
watch it seal itself inside. It will come forth transformed
—a new creature. And in the freedom of its flight you
can rejoice to see the change.

Accept the spirit of adventure in My Spirit. Look forward
to necessary change. My children must resist no move
which takes them farther into experience. They must not
cleave to patterns known, however pleasant. They must be
ready to drop off skins of past awareness and association
as the caterpillars do, and face the new with all their re-

ceptivity alert and capable of growth. There is stagnation in remaining where you are longer than needed for learning, for serving, or for resting to recapture poise. Then the soul must move!

Some lose a lifetime's evolution by the temptation to settle into ease of circumstance. But I would have the pleasant *safely* used. It can provide a wider service for those who learn the balance of response—flexing to ease, stiffening against stress.

And so I say, rejoice in beauty, and in what is made agreeable for you, but do not tremble when the scene must shift. Stand in the wings and watch the stage as it is being set for the next act. Stand in the wings of Conscious Presence and have full confidence. Allow the wonder of My sense of timing to become your own. I could restrain impulsive action which My friends enjoined, or I could march towards danger when they wanted Me to stay. But timing was the essence in each case. I *knew*! And you can know *in* Me.

Daniel could wait, preparing silently the strengths he would be called upon to show before the king. But he could also act with dauntlessness, even when it meant a lions' den. Remember that security lies in obedience to what is right and willed from God, moment by moment, known in the inner chamber of the being which is ruled by Him.

And so I tell you: relax to knowledge of events which come. Anticipate the necessary changes and rejoice. Walk lightly, in the Light—with knowing but no dread. Then you can go from task to task, whether in the outer form of service or the unseen form of prayer and thought, with great effectiveness.

As ritual of acceptance of necessary change, let eye and heart observe the ways of nature. Watch the clouds. Follow the progress of the sun across the sky. Remember changes of the seasons. Think of developing plant, of growing child. Feel the changes in your own body which life processes direct: the pulse, the circulation of the blood, the quiet coming of the breath from outer atmosphere to inner world. Contemplate the beauty of each movement from what has been to what is now, to what shall be. Accept the rhythm of on-goingness and find it good. . . .

Transformation

*But we all, with open face beholding as in a glass the
glory of the Lord, are changed into the same image
from glory to glory even as by the Spirit of the Lord.*
II CORINTHIANS 3: 18

BEFORE THE time of trouble, each who aspires to sonship
will have learned, by Alchemy of Christ, to be a transformer—first, of any harmful thing which touches him.
Later, breathing upon a wider arc, he can protect his
brothers and the animals and growing things, and quicken
even stones beneath his feet. When all sons are formed,
there will be a work of change upon the elements.

Until that time, the alchemy must be a secret power in
each man's being so that he can breathe the damaged air
and drink the poisoned waters and eat the food which
carries seeds of death, and not be harmed.

Yet every sensible care should be employed and no test
made for sake of power alone—no casting down from
temple roof to prove unless it be required. We need not
fear the test, but must not seek it. Pride is the subtlest
form of poison we must watch for while we learn to draw
our nourishment from an environment no longer whole-
some, as bees bring honey forth from what is less than
pure.

This is secret work, interior development, the growing
of new qualities in physical organs; for the body itself
must be quickened to perform the transmutation. Each

major gland must be allowed to do its proper and pre-destined part. Long they have been abused and kept restricted in their functions. Man lost his Eden-image when the glands were blocked from a direct infilling of Light, but they can be reopened to Light, restored as "sons" of God, conscious of Presence, units of radiance, shining from centre as the sun itself.

This is not too much to claim for man as he can be again. When we look at weakness in ourselves or look about at the enfeebled world, we think this is misleading zeal. Look *up*! The Son of God has shown us in the mountain time of His Transfiguration that we *can* know this. "Greater the works *because* I go unto the Father." Transfiguring Light, the purifying Fire of Heaven, can so blaze within the physical cells of dedicated sons that nothing will prevail against them. They will stand.

No, it is not too great a promise to believe. We dare not fail to believe it, every whit.

Yet, even so, we may think that presently our lives do not allow such consciousness to be sustained. Perhaps if it were possible to make some kind of spiritual retreat the ideal could be reached, but hardly in the midst of daily stress. . . . It was in the busy, worldly household of the king that Daniel practised disciplines of simple eating, faithful worship, and personal integrity. Whatever our conditions, it is possible to learn to be self-healing and impervious to anything untoward that would impinge upon or enter into us.

There follow specific means for this. They are: suggestions for suitable food, how to prepare the skin to be protective cloak, a way of using breath and directing certain functions of the glands, a kind of visualization which leads to knowledge of transmuting power, and, finally, the process of Christ-Chemistry which produces Radiance.

REGARDING FOOD:

Daniel "purposed" in his heart not to defile his body with the king's unwholesome foods. This discipline preceded what was granted in those higher powers by which he penetrated a dimension not accessible unless the vehicles of physical being and of mind be freed of dross from self-indulgence. And now for each unit of mankind —yet on the widest scale—such "purposing" is demanded by the fact of mass pollution.

Thus the requirement of personal purity is of a higher order than to indulge man's precious sense of self. Few of us realize this. We are careful to cleanse the vessels in which our food is placed. How much more necessary is purity for the vessel in which the spirit rests. We cleanse the outer surfaces of skin, but allow the body to suffer want of cleanliness within. Flow-through of the transmuting powers can never be entire without the freeing of the wastes of disobedient living in the physical realm. There must be cellular mastery within.

In the usual individual, cells are dying faster than they are restored. To combat the pollution of the present world we must first learn how to even this proportion

59

and then move to a condition of abundant life in which the ratio of living cells exceeds the dying ones. Ultimately man will be able to defeat the need for death and conquer the "last enemy".

Cells that are purified by living foods of earth attract the radiance which they can bear. When the body can support the Everlasting Light, the Light will fall upon the waiting one. Then you will be "instructed" in your frame and over-shadowed there. The Ray of illumination leads from Source straight into marrow structure—into marrow lines of light.

Mankind has slipped into habits of desire for foods and practices which are not of Me. They weigh down; they clog and dull. Return to foods which are natural and can quicken. You will be sustained. Only offer Me the discipline, the love of doing it. Then see what follows.

The Word was made flesh *in* Me, and *from* Me into every son who will. The Word is meant to live, to BE in each, but It must find Its proper food within. The living Word must feed upon the substance of the created one that It may come to BEing in that one.

When we set out to learn about "the living foods of earth", we can find abundant information in books on natural diets but we should avoid the extremes which are sometimes proposed, nor should we follow slavishly the first rules we may happen to read. There must be willing-ness to select our own best regimen by personal quest. Some have need for fasting to prepare. Some will make a gradual change from complex, heavy foods to those which are more natural and sound. Some will alter all false habits at once. Some will still cook; some will eat only what is fired by sun. But it is food from which essential life is not removed that nourishes man in ways which strengthen soul as well as body. A lifeless vegetable diet is scarcely better than a lifeless one of meat. The goal is to be able to attune directly and be quickened daily. "Sufficient unto the day"—*this* day—"our daily bread."

When we undertake the disciplined will-to-purify, we should expect a period of intense inner change. The body is felt to alter from day to day, and this can be bewildering. Sometimes at the outset there is even heightened sensitivity to the very forces we sought to avoid. But we need not fear. By pressing on, dominion is achieved and mastery attained in levels of Light.

It is important to remember, also, that the seemingly intangible attitudes and commitments we have been urged to keep, are creating actual tissue changes which—although not palpable—can make the difference between readiness and unreadiness for the coming test.

Earth and water, air and fire: man's body is made of the four elements. It must be fed from them. Food has full, nourishing power when eaten with awareness that it comes from primal elements and is "prepared" *within* by Holy Fire. This is a process, long stultified, of inner alchemy, but try to imagine its accomplishment in each physical cell; the Presence there of Son-of-Man can do this thing.

The skeletal part of the body corresponds to earth. The foods which represent this element are grains and fruit, leaves, nuts, and roots. Let them be felt to be the flower and fruit of earth, and thus become a form of marrow nourishment.

For the fluid body, whatever other liquid may be taken, have enough of water.

A way of breathing, described later in this section, makes of air an actual food which can be "served" to satisfy the third element of the body.

(Honey is essentially an air food. It should be savoured with the thought of bees in hovering flight upon the flowers of earth. It is a holy food combining all the elements in part. Its wondrous alchemy is of the ultimate fire. It does not spoil in storage. It has been taken through the furnace of its change. Read deeply of the bee's experience of sacrifice.)

And for the fiery element, the fourth, there are oil and wine in ceremonial form.

Seed, and fruit (which is the clothing of the seed), and oil and wine (which are the sacrifice of these)—do you see the beauty of simplicity in patterns made for man? He need not struggle so. He will not struggle so in the New Day.

To make of eating a true sacrament is the important thing. Every breath, each mouthful of food—if rightly taken into being—brings wellbeing. Some eat an apple with no thought of what it is. Some eat it sacramentally, conscious of the wonder of its life, aware of blossoming and growing time, the moods of every weather it has known and the coming of its life within one's own.

As the habit of sacramental eating grows, desire for synthetic foods is drawn away. Natural foods become the only palatable ones. And as the concept deepens in significance, we find less quantity is needed. There is assimilation of new order and degree. Strength flows from less, and less remains to be accounted waste. A particular dross, inherent in earthly matter, is consumed as a fiery emanation even before it reaches the digestive tract and this makes possible absorption of higher energy.

Food should be blessed for its own sacrifice of form, and offered to become the rising power of the next form of life in man, for sake of Presence there! As grace for sacramental eating, one might say: "I am thankful for this food, exemplifying sacrifice. Let it become substance within me for the risen Christ."

Then eat with joy! There must never be a ponderous solemnity in one's effort to sustain this attitude. Evolved thanksgiving is the key to Grace. Grace is the joyful experience of perceptible Light in bodily being.

REGARDING SKIN:

The skin must become a protective garment, as the holy men of the Himalayas know. Oil has a stalwart part. Oil is one of the natural foods of enlightened man. Taken within, it is the fuel for furnace of the spirit. It consumes and is consumed. There is an interchange at point of glands which science will observe in time, but children of the Son will need no proof.

Oil is also natural for the skin as cloak, and is true

mantle. There should be anointing as one goes to bed. Obedience to this will bring instruction, as well as excellent sleep. It need be merest film, but should be placed entire, beginning at the feet. It should be spread upon the skin with thought of all the suns which fell upon the seed or fruit in growing time to fill it with the secret strength and power to embody light in golden essence.

Let oil become the kindling-symbol of alchemy, as well as of the Presence—of insulation and protection, as well as of the Light. Think towards the Form whose very flesh shone in transcendence on the Mount, and say: "It is only because You approach Yourself in us that we are able to approach You in ourselves. As You are sun-Being, Son of God, we can be sun-filled and Son-infilled." For we must be of sun to be a dwelling place for Son. Skin imbued with sun and light is vessel for receiving Him. Spirit within is felt to reach the very edge of skin, fully embodied. This can be a perceptible experience, an important one. Let it come.

In the morning, in bath of water, or dry bath of friction, by hand or towel or brush, let great activity be brought to the skin's surface and be felt as the recharging of its energies.

Stretching movement—tensing and relaxing as animals do—is instinctive wisdom. Let this, too, be part of the brief ritual of beginning day. These acts consume small time but have great merit.

Breath . . . Holy breathing. Feel the Breath of God generated at the point of heart. Feel it change the blood to lighted power. Feel it leave to course through arteries and illumine every cell. We must be permeated by the Breath of God and let its Fire redeem each particle of being. First it must free what is less than free, and then surround and make impenetrable the physical sheath. For the Breath of God, which first brought soul to man, will bring us full protection against a threat to soul.

And He breathed *into* them the breath of life—the first borning. And He breathed *on* them to bestow the Holy Spirit—the second borning. Those of the two *become* the third—and this is son of Son!

Breathe from the deeps of being. Pull in His Holy Breath as roots of giant trees reach out to draw their strength from widest arcs beneath. Tap ever farther circles of awareness for infilling. Let each cell breathe from Be-ing.

Deep breathing, yes, but not a strenuous sort—not a mighty surge of air brought in with effort. Deep breathing *because* the deeps of being recognize the Source of breath—a first creation time of such oneness with Creator that the being breathes *from* Him. It can be gentle and seem not to draw much physical air, but it will permeate the centre of the cells.

Air can carry darkness or great light. *Let* there be light within each cell by day or night, in praise or tribulation.

65

Be sufficient in the power of Holy Breath. This is the Breath that can raise up the temple in three days. This is the Breath that constantly sustains. This is the Breath of the transformers in New Day who will be able to multiply substance by breathing into a consciousness of intense, interior Light.

REGARDING RADIANCE:

Think of the animals of earth, and fish of water, wonderfully adapted to their native elements . . . Think of the bird, creature of air; large chambers in its bones are reservoirs of air to make it light in skeletal form, and the proportionately large heart enables its strong thrust into the heights.

Then think of one adapted to the element of fire! Man of New Day—taken through fire, born into Fire, able to stand in Light. For this he now prepares. This is the reason for the physical acts enjoined as forms of building into readiness. Whole man must be so quickened that he can contain, as well as live within, the element of Fire-of-Spirit.

The centres for transforming power are mouth, heart, and feet. The tongue is quickened in the times of praise, the heart in the Communion rite of Wine, Bread, and Oil —and the feet by rite of Brotherhood, as lived in its compassion and humility towards others in the Father-hood of all.

Light is the agent. It enters through the centres of the head, but is not turned to use until action of the mouth and heart and feet can be unlocked by attitudes realized from lively rites thus given.

The feet become the deep, subconscious knowers. There God's inherent Pattern is imprinted at the base of being, and the energies which pass across it in the circulating stream of Light, are touched each time by evidence of the Plan for Wholeness. Heart is the constant bridge over which the forces pass, and tongue is given power to change any entering negative to positive good. Thus man stands vertical—a pulsing upright of the holy cross —and his arms extend towards other men in blessing, and his feet are sandalled in the gospel of true peace.

The centres of etheric energies, the glands, are actively directed by man's soul when he allows his recognition to bear upon them. In the unaware they work as best they can, bewildered and restricted, but bodily management should be allocated to them consciously, with appreciation for their wisdom and their faithfulness.

At the outset it is well to perform this delegation of authority in detail, considering all organs and activities specifically. In time it can be left to the major departments —fluids, muscles, nerves—or else to the systems of assimilation and elimination. Ultimately, the master gland-of-being can be put in charge by conscious word, relating it to powers of the sun, for *serving* Son, so that one moves in confidence throughout the day in perfect state of health. In New Jerusalem it will be thus.

Indeed, this will be a significant ritual in New Day. No one would think to enter morning hours without a grace for these superior servants of his being and a "conference" with them. Nor would he be content to leave day hours and go into the night without thanking them again and speaking of their tasks of restoration during sleep. In these ceremonies of the dawn and dusk, sons will be recharged from battery of Son, the illumined One whom they know is standing there.

In New Day the arts will also be well recognized as vivifying means: dancing and rhythmic forms of movement for blood circulation and the fluid body; painting and sculpture for flesh and structured part; music for the etheric body of Light. These will all combine in the full spirit of ritual and make of life itself a beautiful expression of totality—the ritual of the creature, living unto the Creator.

Meanwhile, ritual in personal life prepares a man to utilize transforming energies, and quickens and sustains their powers.

Indeed, total transformation is itself a ritual but it is also Way! I AM the Way into this dimension of experience.

In Me your being is surcharged and kept in perfect peace. In Me is perfect flow of energy for all that is your proper work. In Me is food-assimilation, mind-wisdom, and heart-peace.

We go deeper now. The skin is the outermost boundary of tangible, physical form; bone marrow is the opposite pole of inmost being. When the one is touched, the

68

other reached by conscious Fire, they are made impervious and self-restoring. When we relate properly to others in our thoughts and feelings, our skin is changed. Marrow is quickened when we relate properly to Christ. This is the axis of surrender, the polarization of the two great Laws of Love as they affect physical tissue.

Radiation fall-out is the negative energy resulting from man's abortive and self-motivated use of cosmic powers. It *can* be changed to Light. Each particle can be transformed, *beginning in the body of each son*. There the charge of negative can meet the positive of true dedication in an actual alchemy of radiation. It then ceases to damage and becomes an energizing factor to protect and emanate as transforming Light.

Pollution must be fought within the marrow of the bones. The life force there is challenged by the force of death. Begin now to sense the marrow. Learn to feel Light and Life and quickening Fire within. It is not from mind that power to change goes forth, but from the Light-Frame, from the Form *within* the structure. Visualize the skeleton and then see within it the transfiguring framework of the lines of Light in marrow. Make this real.

Now see this not only as Light, but as a form of radiation. Believe that it is good, and that it is strong enough to act for good against damaging radiation. Visualize it first in faith that you may learn to experience it in reality.

As the transforming Blood is felt to circulate through arteries and veins when there is true identification in the

69

Eucharistic rite, awareness of the Fire of Transfiguration makes it possible to feel the Light-Body circulating through the marrow. *This is Radiance.*

Radiance conquers radiation. It will do this literally. Conscious Fire, Element of the invincible, posited in bone and marrow, agrees in essence with the Form of the Overcomer and attracts It there. Being of the same substance with the Light of etheric Presence, there is a magnetic drawing together, and in the circle of Light which the two bodies form, radiation of lower level or degree is powerless. This is the law of superior energy which man will come to know and live by in New Day.

In the king's prophetic dream, "the stone that smote the image became a great mountain and filled the whole earth". The spirit-ether Form of Christ will penetrate and permeate all things. He will take possession of every molecule of nature and of man.

And it was said that the wonder of this new dominion would occur in "the time of iron-mixed-with-clay".

Negative radiations, dangerous ones, affect the iron in physical tissue. Iron is associated with the will. Will to God in Light, and the iron of both material and supersensible degree not only moves through bodily tissue properly, but is new-formed within—created in the marrow. From there it works throughout all systems of the body to protect and to restore. Essence of marrow *is* the Will of God. Man, by his surrender in the central-core of will, is entered by the ultimate heat of flame supernal.

Go under the olive tree, *remembering* with Me. There the will of Son of Man was totally transfigured by will-to-God, and structure changed to Radiance in the tomb!

Behold, the physical body of my willing ones is actually pierced by Rod of Light and Fire—by Rod of Initiation, Rod of Iron! The stab of Rod of Iron inserts the Body of Light within and every particle of being is then fused with It.

So it is that when the supernal Body of Light is one with the physical body of man it attracts the etheric form which corresponds. It literally draws the Form of the Fourth!

After the experience of penetrating Fire to bring the conscious quickening of the Radiant Body within, there must be conscious willingness to sense Radiance without. . . .

Within, without. . . . Though man cannot conceive why so, this is the greater thing to look upon and bear—to stand and see My Being full beside.
One sees the Form of Overcomer with eyes of faith because the marrow of his bones is made of Light.
How fanciful this seems in words to read, but it is supreme reality.

Imagine. Envision. SEE. Walk with awareness of the Radiant One.

Priests of the Age of Fire—and this each one of us is called to be—must know the Son as Master of the Fire of Overcoming. What has been done in Him, is done in His if they can call in faith upon His BEingness within their very bones. Fire in the marrow resists destruction from the lesser fires of man.

This is the force which, in New Age, will change the physical appearance of mankind. There will be luminosity inside the bones so that the skeletal form is evident from without as well.

Desideratum for us even now is transparency—so much light that it flows *through*. "And the prince of this world (darkness, indeed) cometh and findeth nothing in Me", the Christ, and nothing in the sons of Light,— nothing to tie his shadow to and hold. . . .

"Let the light that is in me be Light" is a prayer of great empowering. For lo, My Light shineth in dark places and is brightest there.

"If thine eye be single, *thy whole body will be filled with Light*" . . . This is a literal picture of the one in whom the Name is known—the Name of Lo, I AM . . . Lo, I am with you *even* unto the end of the age—the man-polluted age of self-willed arrogance, using the forces of life for ways of death.

Thus does the furnace lead to transfiguration. The furnace *is* transfiguration in a certain sense. Begin to link the two. *Live* the transfiguration! Live the furnace, live the burning-ground. Know that the dross is being consumed.

The way of preparation is made plain within each one who would be son. In him is diviner in the highest form:

direct knowledge of the truth of his own being. This is the spirit of interpretation as Daniel knew it, as man is meant to know. He shall know his proper food; the modes and means for bodily cleansing; the herbs and ways of earth and water which he needs for healing; the pattern of exercise for full wellbeing; the kind of clothing which does not block inflow of Light. And for the transformation of the evils which assail him from without, his bodily members will be empowered and taught to do the work. What is unfriendly in his food will be transmuted on the tongue of one who stands in perfect praise. By Breath of Union, and anointed with the oil of total dedication, a son is sheathed against the poisoned elements of air, of others' negative will in thought or act, or anything untoward which bears upon him from without. By Light of the transfiguration he will see the intended Plan for all mankind, with clear perception of his particular role within the Plan; and—as ultimate enablement—the reality of the etheric Presence of the Form of the Fourth —which is the *knowledge* of the Christ for Kingdom-Age.

Discipline and faith and will-to-God. These are the essences of inner flame. One need not feel a great exultation to achieve it. One must BE in the quiet confidence of Shadrach, and of Meshach when they stood before the threatening king and faced the furnace door.

Look into the furnace. See the test, Then *see* the shining Form who walks within. See the Great Ones Who attend as well. Their swords are drawn—Archangels. So little there is which man must do himself.

Prepared in body, readied in mind and heart, obedient in faith, he can be as "careless" as the three who said, "If it be so . . ."

Behold the Image of the Transformer. Behold the Image which can stand in fire. This is the Form of the Fourth—our Lord, the Christ . . . Son of God . . . perfected Son in all . . . Seed of new Adams who will be the citizens of Kingdom-Come.

Kingdom Come

Nevertheless we, according to his promise, look for new heavens and a new earth wherein dwelleth righteousness. II PETER 3: 13

Now I will tell you a higher thing, and it will be to you a remembering and a return to what was known before.

But the uses shall be for this time, and the uses shall be for a time to come.

And understanding of it will fall upon the people as a mantle upon the shoulders of the world;

And they will kneel and worship truth in the spirit of understanding.

Truth shall be within their beings and in their acts.

Truth shall be in their goings and comings and in their speaking to each other.

And the government shall be upon My shoulders, saith God, the Son!

THIS IS the way that man will live in the New Day—in Kingdom Come. The mighty purging will have cleared away the chaff. The tempest will have blown from off the earth the cruelty and infidelities. Man will stand as child of Heaven and as son of God, after the Form of the Fourth, in image of His own. . . .

The New Day, New Jerusalem, will be peopled by illumined ones. They will have passed the time of Fire and thus prepare, by their earth living, a place where those who come for evolution not experienced before may find it easier to grow. Man can no longer bear his separatism, but neither could he bear communal life that does not offer perfect freedom for the individual. And such community is not man-made. It comes of God's dominion. When each is perfect in obedience to God, as King, he can be perfect citizen of His Kingdom-Come. Thus men can live in great "combines" with each one served, and serving, in agreement and in light. Each will be led directly of the Spirit and thus be perfectly sustained, perfectly fulfilled, and perfectly related as individual to all others. This is proper commune-ism under God.

The Lighted way will be the natural one when man is son of God, walking the earth redeemed, refined by fire and purified for life in kingdom dwellings. And seed is now placed well into the dark and troubled soil of change. You see the stirring and tormented earth and feel concern for suffering men. But this must be. There is new life, deep planted. Leaf will come. The time is near enough to say "Behold" and open eyes in those who will be here to greet that Day.

There will be beautiful simplicity of dress. Man will be clothed as angels are. Colours not yet realized will be a gift of light, delighting eye and spirit. Each son will have a colour of his own as evidence of his heart's agreement, and each shall design his individual robe by fact of essence, but there will be those assigned to aid in the making of the garment. Weaving will be an exquisite art, a highly favoured one. Fabric will not wear away as it does today. It will change into new form and colour as the consciousness of wearer changes. Stones will adorn, but not for prideful use. According to the owner of the robe, stones will be integral part and create interchange of energies between him and the outer atmosphere. The girdle will be ample and will hold the elements of a kind of consecration not yet known, peculiar to each man.

There will be dancing in that Day and man's apparel must not restrict. It will have flow, grace, beauty . . . and he will move in rhythm with the elements of earth and sky. There will be winter rhythms and the joy of spring. His garments will be changed accordingly; yet be his own in evidential ways. (It will not be "winter" in terms of cold: quietness . . . fallow time for deepening of forces from within, and springtime for the coming of new growth.)

Change will occur in everything, but change grown out of restoration of the good from ages past to marry what is known of wisdom now. By symbol will values from the past be carried forward, with none of the sterility of curious investigation as made by scholars who turn superficial mind upon the quest. They catalogue and label, but when heart is ready, Higher Mind instructs and man will *know* what was concealed in signs of earlier time. He will be cautious of discarding ancient lore. In it are yet great truths for the children of New Day.

There will come total use and total understanding of all that earth was meant to be for man from God. The depths will yield their secrets, what is hidden be revealed.

77

Nature will open as a book to be read with reverence, and on every page be as clear in its relationship to man's soul forces as to his material form.

By the Light of the Transfiguration, men will scan the records of pure state of being and recall the forms which satisfy that state, and by the power of disciplined will-to-God, *see* into being the creations of New Day—New Day returned to day as at beginning.

New Age will be the age of transfiguration—the return of giant forms Who have received the Light, and the preservation of initiates who abide . . . they will both hear and speak the Word, and earth will be renewed to garden grace. Process of regeneration will be drawn from inherent core of recorded energy. "Destroy this temple and I will raise it up again!" Men of transfiguration will be able to restore any loss within themselves, and turn and look upon destruction of earth forms and "see" them brought again to first perfection. For the pattern of first-fire resides in everything God made and saw and has called "good". Each son is unit of transforming power *because* in each the Son is centred there.

By his obedience Noah saved the seeds of life for multiplying forms after the water passed across the earth. But after fire, the forms themselves will seem to be destroyed and the obedient ones must be the agents of restoring them from very essence. They must have faith and power to speak their "Let!" with thunder from the mount of quickened vision.

And even now, as an act of will, we should practise

visualization of this lifted kind. Look upon a seed, or leaf, or flower, or any living thing and *see* it. Then look away and learn to hold the image clear and whole as if it were still seen with physical eye. Children of New Day will do this work—a form of "Let" allotted only to those of purified intent.

It will be simpler, less complicated than you might think now. Remember: the wheat will be the remnant saved; chaff will be gone. It will not be the world you see today. Those who remain—or come!—will have the spirit quickened and made pure. Motives will be single unto God and from Him unto man again in love.

Man will return to crafts—to work of his hands, but not as done before. Thought will be the energy, and dedication will be the source of patterns and design. Worship will precede knowledge. Man will kneel to know, and then will *think* to do. What he beholds in inspiration he will accomplish by his thought. He will be faithful to the "vision received upon the mount". He will have learned that only what is guided can be safe and strong. He will not dare to build without the Builder's plan.

For the crisis will force acceptance of man's accountability for having disregarded rights of air and soil and water, and for harm done vegetable and animal life in all its forms. Some of this he will redeem by dedicated effort, as has been shown, but first redemption will be through grace—a holy thing which falls upon the earth as dew, and in the twinkling of an eye has purified the *seed*. Then man's work can begin again under the law of love. Under

Heaven's Government, in Kingdom-Come, he will begin again, cleansed in attitude and purpose, chastened by tribulation, standing in robes made white by cosmic Fire. After the furnace, man will serve in fear as fear is truly meant. He cannot then be careless of the rights of any living thing. He will see holy life in everything.

In that Day he will learn many ways to bring perfection into body and estate, but he will learn because he turns, as son, to Source of knowledge. Instinctive knowledge will again be his. The cells of inner being will discern directly. No man need teach another. Each will *know*. This is the covenant proclaimed so long ago: "After those days, saith the Lord, I will put my laws in their inward parts, and write it in their hearts; and will be their God, and they shall be My people. And they shall teach no more every man his neighbour and every man his brother, saying know the Lord; for they shall all know Me from the least of them unto the greatest of them saith the Lord; for I will forgive their iniquity, and I will remember their sin no more" (Jer. 31: 33, 34).

For every aspect of the earth to be redeemed—of mineral, herb, or creature—there will be a human group assigned to channel will-to-purify. This is the work of ritual, inspired by Those of higher consciousness.

After the Fire a ritual is full of Very Life. Then man will be given forms as were the priests of old, and in them will be power beyond the form—quickened again as ceremonies were when they began. In ritual will the past relive its wisdom and project its power, but it will not be dead unto the new. Behold all ages meet in this New Day. Each brings its best and each shall be fulfilled in union before the King of men, Son of the Most High God. . . . Colour, symbol, sound, and movement join in potency; nothing is without high significance, known by the temple ones in early times—now to be known again for this New Day.

There will be rituals of transmutation so that all matter is transformed and offered back as it began when it came forth from *LET*!

And Holy Breath will be the energy. And Holy Fire will fall upon the altar as the shaper and the shield. And each shall be perfected as a part of Whole—Image of God entire, with man, as son, only little lower than the bright angelic Ones.

The ritual of Holy Breath will be the first for purification of the earth after the wind and flame have passed across the land. And those who have chosen to let Him walk with them—the Form of the Fourth, the Very Son of God—will be the transformers after fiery test. Their breath, their being, will directly purify the elements. From eye and mouth and nostril will come forth the power to change the molecules around their presence. The breath that leaves a body thus recharged can fall in blessing upon anything within its range. And when a band of Breathers of the Holy Breath breathe together in ritual upon a point of need, there shall be full regeneration. Quickening shall come, indeed, and in the twinkling of an eye . . . instant of flow of Holy Breath. . . .

Round, with centre open to the sky, will be the temple built for breathing Holy Breath.

And for regeneration of the holy forms from structures of earth which have been sullied by man's lack of dedication, the temples will be rectangular like those of early Greece.

Construction of these new, true temples will be rapid, following *thought*—on earth as it *is* in Heaven! Do you see? Thus the importance of purity of thought. It is the substance, the material used. They must build well . . . build pure and strong foundation, wall and roof. Make beautiful the passageways and the approaches. Build confidence and trust into the beams. Build attributes into the floors to mount through feet of those who walk thereon. Stones shall speak the truths and men will "hear" throughout their beings. . . .

Try to rejoice in your anticipation of that Day. Let it be real in your extended vision. See it as done upon the earth. Hear the great "Let!" Imagine the rising of the temples into splendid form. Accustom the eyes to "see" the process of construction, observing each detail as it occurs. *Watch* the elements of the structure being placed. Then observe the uses and intent for each.

Schools will be temples of all learning and all art, but *temples*, and it shall be understood that knowledge must be wisdom unto God, unfolding in the manner of children as they learn to play, with joy and purpose evolving outward from the core of an awareness never unrelated to the Source. Learning will be adventure among beneficent forces and the discovery of uses for everything which will be left or newly formed. . . .

In temples for the purpose of bestowing knowledge of nutrition in the highest form, there will be trained ones who have offered spirit-dedication before their minds were turned to study. Their place of work will be a laboratory, but will have an altar at its centre as a heart. There will be those who understand the grasses, every kind, and those who understand each kind of growing thing. New foods will be available, but each must learn what he should choose—Garden of Eden counterpart, indeed! Man will eat "winter" foods and "summer" foods and live in harmony with season once again, though seasons will be changed in an important way. Watch for all the wonders of the physical realm to join their treasures for true worship in New Day. The New Jerusalem will be a lovely land.

Freedom from noise—the sound of Holy Word will then be understood and reverenced. Language of New Day will be the purity of thought in sons made pure in Son Himself.

Temples for silence—creative silence, that music may come from realms beyond earth-waves of sound. . . . Spiralled as a nautilus for music and the heavenly arts . . . towers for science . . . and the great temples which will have one purification aspect for the whole. Different peoples will be adepts for specific roles, but of the *whole*. None will feel rivalry, being certain of his appointed usefulness. The land of Light is for each, and yet for all.

Temple of Fire—the temple of the true relationship of son of man to Son of God. In it will be symbols for the threefold nature of man's relationship to the Holiest, in heart, mind, and will—and WILL will be the headstone of the three! There will be wall paintings of the sacrifices —the great and cosmic one of Sacrifice of Essence into form, and those throughout the ages . . . Abraham and Isaac . . . all the first-fire evidences . . . furnace and Crucifixion . . . each ending in its victory, in supreme defeat of what is not of sun, of Son, of Fire Celestial. . . .

And so there will be man of the New Age, adapted to the element of Fire—taken through fire, born into Fire, able to stand in Light. Shekinah will be upon him and within, and he will speak the tongues of triumph at the Throne—singing the Song of full awareness in that Day.

And even now we need to hear the echo of that Song so that the sound of conflict and invasion not overwhelm us when our testing comes. We must know that only good stands in essence after the fire has played across the whole. Flames of change consume only what binds.

Crises and war, tribulation . . . these are means of making man a son. They come not of the will of an angry God, but as a form of processing. Of course we wince to know the pain ahead, but even through pain we look upon the pictures of the life to be when pain has done its work. Kingdoms of man must fall. Monuments he makes to any other gods must have crumbled before he will be willing to erect the Image of the Son of God within his heart. Heart-humility precedes the bending of

84

the mind, but both must bow before the coming of the Lord. Then man himself will be the symbol of the Cross. The sacrifice accepted is complete.

Earthquakes . . . fire of earth will meet the Fire of Heaven. Men will quail to feel the heat of trembling earth and ask that caves be opened for protection. But there will be no hiding place except the heart of dedicated will. Only in attitude of "If it be so" will man find shield, and it must be the pure desire for Will-of-God that God be not betrayed by child, His creature. Then creature-child is son, indeed, and meets the Son in very truth, and can contain Wonder within, greater than anything without. Those who go towards furnace with this thought of God will see the Form of the Fourth within the flames and not be troubled by a fire heated seven times hotter than the fire of any previous age of cleansing.

Give praise before it comes! Daniel gave praise as well as prayers of supplication. Praise is the way of prophets who behold the outer coming of events. Praise is the way of Kingdom's children who know in inner being the conditions over which His Government will reign: harmony, love, opportunity, abundance, right use of all forces. . . . We can live *now* in consciousness of these, in the beauty and peace of our anticipation of that lighted time when Christ-Messiah comes to BE among His own, to be *within*, *without*, in fullness unto men. It is more than needful that we do, for each must grow to sonship before the greater kingdom of sons can find the laws of Kingdom living under the Father-King. And each bright principle of harmonious living must be grasped and honoured ere a man be son. Thus he begins to live the laws before he sees them lived by other men. He does not wait, saying, "When all live unto God I will conform . . . when the world allows me I will be righteous". Alone he wears the breastplate (of righteousness) in order that he meet the ultimate Right in other men. He lives *in* image as Image of the One. When all are Image, they will behold the King Himself, orbed and complete, Whole of created One for this sun-plane. There *is* a King to rule the Kingdom Come, and He will be the One found within the furnace— the Form of the Fourth, the Very Son of God.

And so we live now in awareness of the Kingdom which shall come when test is passed by man—not as unreal escape from times which are, but as promise and projection which are the energies of fulfilment. Let joy mount as we foresee the joy of that Day when men abide by laws put into their hearts by God. The sense of its completion before it has occurred is seal of overcoming. "It is finished" was said in moment of the most intense appearance of defeat! Seal this on the inner eye. This will be the mark upon the forehead in that day!

The test will come, but we hear the wondrous promise: "Lo, I am with you *even* unto the end of the age." When hearts would surely fail, knowing the utter frailty of man against the nether works of man himself, the Form of the Fourth will have come within, that He may walk beside . . . *even* unto the end . . . the end of darkness . . . unto the Age of Light . . . thence to His Kingdom Come.